asphalt CIGAR

KEVIN | CONNOLLY

asphalt CIGAR

COACH HOUSE PRESS

Published with the assistance of the Canada Council, the Ontario
Arts Council, the Department of Canadian Heritage and the
Ontario Publishing Centre.

ACKNOWLEDGEMENTS
Some of these poems have appeared, or will appear, in the following publi-
cations: *Who Torched Rancho Diablo?, What!, narc, 1cent, Exile, Mental
Radio, Rampike, West Coast Line, CB, Arc,* and *Crash.*

"Columbus Day" was published in chapbook form under the title
Christopher Columbo, in 1992 by Contra Mundo Press. Earlier versions of
"Progress Report," "Critique of Good Intentions," "Asphalt Cigar," and
"Proof" appeared in *Deathcake,* (Proper Tales Press, 1991) and *Pterodactyls*
(Pink Dog, 1988). Warm thanks to all of these small press editors for
encouragement, editorial advice, and support.

Thanks to Michael Ondaatje for "first contact," Mike Redhill for good faith,
Gord Robertson for good eyes, and gary barwin, Fred Gaysek, Frank Davey,
Steve McCaffery, Clint Burnham, Nestor Kruger, Karen MacCormack and
Lillian Necakov for friendship, guidance, and good advice.

Special thanks to Gillian Adamson and Stuart Ross, who see everything,
and my editor, Lynn Crosbie, for service above and beyond.

First Edition
Printed in Canada
1 3 5 7 9 8 6 4 2

Canadian Cataloguing in Publication Data

Connolly, Kevin
Asphalt Cigar

Poems.
ISBN 0–88910–469–7

PS8555.)66A76 1995   C811'.54   C95–930765–6
PR9199.3.C65A76 1995

"There's a fine line between fishing
and just standing on the shore like an idiot"
Steven Wright

I ASPHALT CIGAR

II COLUMBUS DAY

III NOTES TOWARDS A REVISED
   BIOGRAPHY OF FRIEDRICH
   NIETZSCHE

asphalt
CIGAR

ASPHALT CIGAR

O, the heartbreak !
The mean transistor,
the incontinent sponge of faith.
A hereditary passing
from parent to offspring—
you were born with these relations,
mental leaps, associations:
the militant thugs,
the multilingual polyglots.

The bridge over this city,
specializes in heavy transit;
trucks and vans carrying
baked goods, trucks delivering
other trucks and vans....
The city is swollen with defeat;
each lung has its bachelor apartment,
nothing crosses over.

You've been falling slowly
through the faltering air,
you've been falling
in this lifelong sink,
oiled and swirling,
overlooked by luxury motor lodges.
At last a way jumps clear
into your glazed lenses.

I might even let you follow it—
time's syncopated sludge-drum.

Ju jubes, glop, an ardent
prayer: the sum-trickling
wealth of civilization
lies ogling your spirited feet.

PASSION D'AMOUR

The pavement rumbled with the dove, then dusted itself
and grabbed a sandwich before the cocktail party, the hook of its
nose gathering the crunching crumbs left by distracted
secretaries named Jean and Amanda, who, over lunch, were
stunned by the Christophe Lambert look-alike waiter from the
Italian Bistro across the street, so sexy as he contemplated suicide
at the moment his dour reflection caught in the glint of the
businessman's knife, glanced off the darkened window of the
hurtling driverless taxi, and struck the dumbfounded women at
eye level, like friction-generated electricity, or a gift of handcut
crystal, picked discerningly from a catalogue, wrapped
individually in tissue, then shipped halfway across the globe to
be packed in recycled wrapping, brought nervously to the
housewarming party, and shoved in a jealous rage in the vulgar
bride's sneering face by the guest, who, having lost her man, was
unwilling to submit gracefully to further humiliation.

CRITIQUE OF GOOD INTENTIONS

Hey! You with the hair!
Turn up the sunlight, I'm in
the mood for a little philosophy.

The meaning of it all
drops through my head like a
coupon through a mailslot,
wet bread sliding from a dirty plate.

My problem is I can't be serious.
I'll be serious.

Wake up and blush, angry nation!
The shell-shocked islands
of your childhood dreams have
sprouted highballs and t-shirt stands.

And I've been up all night crooning,
wrestling my vainglorious corpuscles.

I've been trying not to give my feelings
other words, trying not to explain to myself
what I mean when I say:

I have lingered in the yellow-toothed dawn...
I have honoured the varicose veins of destiny...

At the end of the hall,
night stands swimming
in its dark blue raincoat.

And you! You with your backs
against the vivid camels,
you understand what I mean
when I say the Life Convinced
and the Life Confused have settled
on the same brute colours.

Certainty arrives, pushing
a pink shopping cart.
The sun glints stupidly
on the peeling sills.
The junk mail never stops arriving.

THEY REMAIN HATLESS

"Marooned" was the wrong word for it.
Say, instead, "stuck" with "this shallow panic."
Not articulate but ... that other thing,
the bald thoughts remain hatless in a

flash flood of monogrammed confetti.
"All Hail," a bored crow offers,
the end, it seems, is close at hand again.
You wear those shallow cuts as

an itinerary of minor renovations, all
your hard thought turned pale and
vanished with the cordless sun.
What's left now is only dark-*ish*

really, not nearly so wild or
impressive as I had hoped.

VACANT

I'm afraid for all the
slim men in empty apartments,
the irritant clatter of their lives
converging on them by boat,
by plane, or rattling in the cold
compartment of a twelve-wheeler
driven into wild weather.

Pity them, squatting on their haunches
like natural men, having forgotten
to take note of things,
to look forward to this.

Their minds are bouncing
with the place settings
in the back of the truck.

They don't know how to
welcome what the space
makes room for—the blue,
searching fingers of the city,
the debutante swish of passing cars,
the power crouching in the sockets,
hanging on their every move.

Sirens swing in like wired angels,
and he's worried about dishes.

BERNIE'S TEARS

There was a lot riding on
the eventual arrival of Bernie's misery,
or on its eventual failure;
but even with the basin below
his would-be tears,
the results proved inconclusive.

Salt water can vanish into blue air.
You remember all the bored courtiers
by name, their exotic pets and
rank gossip decorated the halls.
The sky leaned back against the dry
grass, the dank shadows,
and moaned with indigestion.

For now, let's say misery
is a tossed pot which leaves
the panting memory of the flower.

PLAINSONG

The stars are
little plastic
cheese swords
stuck into the big,
triangle-sectioned,
select-a-flavour,
Gruyère rondeau
of the darkness.

Well ...
that's hardly cause
for celebration.

THE EMPRESS HOTEL

Those were the days of rails and roses,
of women on bridges and at tables,
boys with stilts, and poised girls
on beaches looking out to sea.

The sky comes in on pink waves,
everything like a raised hand
leading back to the beach.

Blown flowers, children in the street
already past their prime.
Popsicles melted in clammy hands,
bicycles run repeatedly against
the spinster's wrought iron.

The baby in the red silk cap,
the mother, her sunglasses, and the dog
snapping at the exposed heels.
Someone shouts, watch it,
watch the child!

and like a red wave
everything runs back up the beach:
from the poised girls with flamingo feet,
to the middle-aged women
drinking draught at the Empress Hotel.

Days weave in and out
like voices in the dark.
They're beyond the yellow doorcracks,

beyond the keyholes, bleeding light.

The easy chairs are lit by television screens.
Women wearing white gloves drinking,
calling to old men through
televisions at the Empress Hotel.

The woman drinks, the children sleep.
She starts before they are awake and
they are asleep before she finishes
and sleeps herself.

And the white women
sing them beyond sleep,
dresses gathered at the ankles

like vines leading back to the beach,
to the bridge, to the girls clearing
tables at the Empress Hotel.

Men's faces swimming in televisions,
eyes full of songs and flashes:
empty mouths and faces, vague ships
drifting in a sea of fire and iron.

Old women whispering at fences,
at hedges in the dark,
whispering: beaches and gloves
and sixty-cent draught. Whispering them
to duty, to pistols and to carts,
songs swirling,

gathering at their ankles like the birds

on the beach, like the women at tables
and on railway overpasses,
rushed moaning under doorcracks
at the Empress Hotel.

Each day wakens with blue precision,
and the years slip away in waves.
They are born, they carry their days
clumsily in handkerchiefs or paper bags.

A sky of bleeding beach.
A gloved keyhole.
Gaunt faces at the television
looking out and looking in,
the cards raised like hands
shouting save it, save it,
pointing to the bridge.

The woman has made her face up
with dark colours.
Blue lips and red lashes,
white gloves and coffee-coloured hair.
She is swaying on her heels,
the belt on her jeans pulled
a notch too tight.
She is swaying on her heels
on the railway overpass.

The red cap, slipping
away like a rose,
the blanket falling and
the red cap slipping away.

The child dropping from the white gloves
and falling from the overpass,
falling through railings and through iron,
through the eyes of the old men
coming on to poised girls
on the beach at the Empress Hotel.

The sky dropping in waves
before they can move
toward the voices shouting,
toward the child
lying on the beach below,
head blown like a rose,
the sea poised,
and the train coming on.

HE DISSECTS THE ALIEN

No one is certain if
she fell or jumped
or the pavement just grew her;
whether she sees herself in this way;
whether her eyes, her tongue,
belong to this, or some other set
of extenuating circumstances.
The pavement is a muddle of endings ...
happy   nerve   sad   surprise
but it's all academic now.
The bottom line is the concrete

has trapped her, for a moment at least,
and there's sufficient light
for a brief tactical examination,
enough edge left in his voice to
gather a modest crowd over
the hissing, spitting, thing.
Figure out how it ticks and
it can't hurt you, is the thinking;
label separate parts so you know where
they all go afterwards. Make sure
the sketches and the depositions jive.

Once gained, never surrender the advantage.

RAW DOUGH
for Arthur Penn

Clyde used to think that if he
looked the bullets in the eye
they'd freeze somehow—like
rodents on a wild highway—
find their own weight and tumble
to the pavement. He sees now
he'd been wrong about all that,
hot metal imploding the car doors,
hammering out the glass in
a few satisfying thuds.
The flight bag on the seat beside
him isn't living up to its name
just now. Inside, bundles of cold
cash in lottery sequence.
From under the dash he tries the dead
engine again while metal wasps fall
through the chassis in horizontal downpour,
all tooth and thick-headed weight.
He rolls over her wet slump,
feeling a handful thrown through
him into her. Before the day goes out
completely he wills the door open
(or is that also the bullets?)
tugging at her feebly as he moves.
The last hope of live escape is
trickling red feathers on the vinyl,
and so Clyde will picture it instead—
an alternative stylish closing:
accidental gunman cutting down
some brilliant evasion, a single

bullet travelling through both hearts,
an end wilder than their wild lives.
The red curtain dropped over rising eyes;
the forest of slender onlookers,
spinning to a stop.

Igot   inspired, just before I wrote this.
Igot   an aunt with a colostomy, we do lunch sometimes.
Igot   one red sock on, and one blue, and a pair
        just like them in the drawer.
Igot   Zee-brick on my bedroom walls.
Igot   Rod Serling's left eyebrow.
Igot   a freezer full of Pogos.
Igot   a jazz pianist who won't fuck off while I sleep.

Igot   a new stanza.
Igot   five guys to screw in my lightbulbs.
Igot   an extra nipple. My last girlfriend found it
        very attractive.
Igot   Scotty's dilithium crystals.
Igot   a William Shakespeare cookie tin.
Igot   a name ...
Igot   a name ...
Igot   a year's supply of Rice-a-Roni, the San Francisco
        treat.
Igot   the Gravy Train, cornered in my bathroom.
Igot   a rather limited imagination.

JUNKMALE

I wonder if we'd all calm down
a little if sex were a seasonal thing,
like fruit ripening. If all you
had to do was sit in the wet dirt
and wait for the carrot to scream.

In my dream, Madonna
is shitty in bed. She's
hard, and kind of boney, and
bellows "Respect Yourself!"
the whole time.

There's a tired-looking waitress
at the bar at the end of the street
who wears shiny low-cut blouses.
She's circled the bar with typewriters,
one typewriter for each gaunt regular.
"One day," she tells me, "One of
these MEN is going to write me
into a novel."

I've just spent the whole fucking night
playing pool with Bob on a threadbare,
half-size, buck-a-play table.

"Research," I call it.
Bob calls it "Thursday,"
and he's right.

TWELVE ARRESTS, NO CONVICTIONS

Tonight I spurned the bingo palace,
circumnavigated the "wrong" preference,
rode the dust in an open car
with a gun between my knees

I couldn't say:
"The night stood me up
like dried pasta,"
and keep a straight face.

There are too many motives
demanding attention.
No one asked me to invent them.
No one's asked me nicely,
at any rate.

"I am not a drowning man."
"I am not a burning building."
The song at least makes sense
and pays for its own lunches.

I won't crouch and mumble
with the atoms of The Greats,
scrape lips from statuettes,
connect the dots and call it home.

I won't play the *gombeen,*
strap peat to my head,
make a petty brushfire
of my ancestry.

I'm prepared to face it—
I'll never share straws
with The Bard.
Some people have no luck with
wood shop or elective surgery;
with me something always
ends up leaking.

I won't quietly accept it:
"to sit with a blind brow
above an empty heart."
I'm not sure I need
to know where empty is.

DON'T PISS OFF THE TRAIN

I'm consoled by this hole
where you once tarried
                    James Tate

Everyone who rides will eventually arrive at
the tireless line. What's harder
is to placate the schedule,
keep the iron veins just so,
tip the umbrella on the cocktail
jauntily, as if it were the last.
There are exceptions,
still, the rules plod on,
devising more attractive corners.

Acknowledge the old flame
who shares your "private berth,"
conquered over lunch, conquered
again, briefly, across
a dark and grainy aisle.
You know she is a figment,
an improbable furnishing
for the observation car.

I've retrained my desires
at each stop; embarked,
offloaded, debriefed, inserted,
and detonated the tortured luggage
of my whims, my accidents.
The dank enlargements,
catalogued and furtive.

I was observed, and swallowed
by the throngs. I listened,
and was taken up in cartoon wisps,
buffeted by tears,
ringing loose and jangly.

I endured those intolerable lectures:
in my ring finger,
in the certain memory
of another infernal body,
in the abject silence
of a poorly mounted buffet.

I forgot the coupons
promising redress,
and so I cowered,
brushed by static breezes.
I address the poisoned ladder
of my fate and default,
returning to a life
of plunder and of want.

THE CONDEMNED MAN

The condemned man steps
from the subway train
and listens for the whistle.
He looks the platform
up and down—one,
two count—then back
to let the doors slide shut.

Today he's monitoring
the yellow alarm strip
running in a line down this car
then picked up, he assumes,
in the next, hovering
above the white hands
of the commuters.

For now, he's the celebrity here,
invisible but unique.

He wears a coat hanger
in the collar of his jacket.
On tiptoes he hooks himself
to the overhead bar,
squeak-swings like a parrot,
kicking off the chairs,
clearing himself some space.

The lawyers are the worst;
suffocating in dry-cleaned
suits, plastic and glaring

bright as car roofs
seen by seabirds
passing over the city
on a too-hot afternoon.

He's got news for these guys—
he's not letting up.

There's no percentage
in going quietly.
The hairs on
his doomed legs
appear above the rented socks,
below the pants cuffs,
rising with his kicking.

His shoes leave smears
on the windows
and the bright handrails,
on the folded wheelchair
of a shaking senior.
Lights dim and hum, another station
slows to a stop.

The prisoner unhooks himself,
shoves his way through
to the waiting door.

They shuffle,
then fan out behind him,
the little cares,
the little lies sighed quietly
into file folders,

into handkerchiefs.
This is how he knows:

no one leaves, no one
even moves to leave.
He alone is listening
for the gasp and thud
of opening doors,
then the whistle after
he takes his single step out.

If not now, then later.
Whichever way they want to work it,
he'll be ready.

THE NEW MAN

In every man is a woman
with a man inside her,
trying to get out.

He agrees to be
handcuffed
during intercourse.

columbus
DAY

I

In Genoa,
Chris sells paintings in the street.
Bullfights, dancing girls,
ships on velvet.
His favourite, silver,
cross on the sail billowing.
He dreams of the sea.

At night Chris piles up
the frames on the wharf,
holds up an empty one to the horizon,
watches the sun set through it,
heart in full sail.

II

Chris has had enough of this.
In the morning it rained
and though the paint held
the velvet crushed and stained.
Someone splashed mud on the silver ship.
Chris scratches off the marks
one by one
with his thumbnail.

Behind him in the street
someone is holding up a postcard,
comparing it to the cathedral.
A dancer appears, multicoloured
like the paintings.
She clicks her
castanets in the clean air.

Chris smiles and she whirls closer.
The castanets clack hard
like clams around his head.
Chris shudders, protects
his ears with his hands.

III

Chris has had it up to here
with velvet paintings.
He books on board a ship,
the *Anna Chronisma.*
On board, too, is young
Vascular da Gama.
He is Chris's nemesis,
though he doesn't know it yet.
They play a lot of shuffleboard.

On the other side
someone thinks he has seen land.
Chris leans over and sees
a branch, a leaf, a dead seagull,
straightens up,
hits his head against the lifeboat.

Out on the earth
the sea heaves like
the dying sighs
of some half-remembered
father.

IV

On land, Chris hits the town.
Yonge Street
with Ponce de Leon
the Spanish queen
Chris meets at the Hotel Isabella.

As Chris has no job
Ponce pawns his brocade
curtains, his silver star,
the lawn ornaments from home.
Chris buys The Radio Mike.
"Sing along with the radio.
You too can be a star."

At night Chris wanders under
the concrete peaks
singing Blue Moon,
The Rain In Spain.
No one is listening.

V

Before long Chris is discovered.
A man passes in the street,
says he has a good voice,
"like pure velvet."
Chris will play six shows
at the Barcelona Bistro—
all the omelettes he can eat.
Da Gama meets him later
and hears the good news.
Chris decides to let him
work the lights.

The room rings
with the sound of spoons.
Chris sings a duet with the radio,
Blue Moon and
The Rain in Spain.
The applause is thunderous.

VI

Years pass
and Chris has lost his edge.
His epaulettes are dirty,
his hair needs washing,
he terrorizes the lighting crew.
He has lost faith,
joined the Flat Earth Society.
Next week he will play The Bistro again
while da Gama plays
The Imperial Room.
Chris sings only
once in a blue moon now.
He lets the radio sing
and mouths the words.

At night Chris hears the sirens
scream across the blue night.
He pulls himself from the window,
buries his face in the covers
until they fade away.

VII

Da Gama meets Chris playing in the street.
He is made up like a king
wearing Chris's first velvet tux
(Chris has pawned it).
Chris now plays the radio for change.
He calls da Gama over,
asks him for a quarter.

Da Gama knocks him to the ground.
Chris reels and rises,
puts the mike between his teeth
and attacks.

Next day they're both deported.
Chris is shackled in the hold
while da Gama plays the ship's lounge
with Chris's radio.

In the hold Chris hears
the clack-clacking of castanets,
the radio piped through
the ship's loudspeaker,
the off-rhythm pounding
of the dancers' feet.
The sea rises and falls
with the sound of his weeping.

VIII

They let Chris keep the handcuffs.
Da Gama can have the microphone,
Chris has no need for it any longer.
He sets up his stall by the wharf.
Velvet paintings,
the skyline of Toronto, Mounties,
portraits of The Great One.

Chris hangs the handcuffs
on a nail by the door.
Sometimes at night,
when he hears the horns
of the outbound ships,
Chris pulls them down
and shackles himself to the dock,
just in case.

notes towards

a revised

biography of

FRIEDRICH NIETZSCHE

I. PRELUDE TO A PHILOSOPHY OF THE FUTILE

Nietzsche is a horse trainer in a Dionysian frenzy. This question of far-sightedness, he has humanized it, presented it as counterfeit beauty. He says the eyes of justice weaken and sadden men. To put up with people, the impersonal ought to get a word in sometimes, must communicate a morality for deaf mutes, not perpetuate the indecent idleness of the psychologist. Even the most courageous among us is a mistake—a pied-piper with a tuning fork.

Out of life's school of war lurch more puffed-up philosophers. A hammer is a declaration of war. Conscience is indecent.

II VALET OF THE IDOLS

I hate Rousseau. I see only one who experienced disgust—in the unreal, in the faith that only what is separate and individual, is an affirmation of any kind. A nihilistic sigh, a paltry excellence and a delight in languages which are inexplicably popular. As altruism is to those who fool themselves, so grammar school drilling is to tremendous, ruthless, external hostility. Contentment is a lucky accident—not peace at all, but depravity; a sick animal lacking a theologian.

In Christianity, the closing of certain public baths encouraged a morbid pride, a hatred of the senses, a fastidiousness with regard to food. Christ is a snake of both sexes, entertaining in a tree. His precious self-assertion stands in opposition to the believer, the madhouse, the gospels, the psychology of conviction.

III. THUS SNAKES SARAH BERNHARDT

They become convalescents in tears, an involuntary mask which
is called "honesty," not in the afterworld, but in the free society,
honestly perpendicular. Whatever there is in me that has feeling
is a hammer sleeping in an ugly stone.

I want it perfect. I want it to rain beauty like a shadow,
a chain withered with little fungi.

Their stopgap blood is roaring, virtuous. Sleeping senses are
heavenly fireworks. I'll gain my pleasure in punishment, justice
will whirr out of their mouths. Their hands are hymns, uprooted
and broken in the sun, their eyes, preachers of equality, of the
"real and apparent world" they want to bite.

IV. HUMID, ALL-TOO-HUMID

Vanity is a gay science, more deeply ingrained than truth or falsehood, and he subscribes to both. To recognize that as a passion, an enthusiastic passion that seeks to seduce him into a fitting poetic expression. He is not made for pity. Genius is not as profound a reverence as high-grade solitude and its poisonous nooks. In a lizard, a lost finger is replaced without love, without cunning and shrewdness, without the long, undismayed forgery that is the repulsive cult of suffering.

Laughing is a risk. Gods, typically, do not enjoy mockery. To press, or to lie still as a mirror buried under dim and thick ice, not having received graces, not having said a word, or cast a glance, or rejoiced at another's expense.

The genius teaches the doltish all that is loud and self-satisfied. Much is gained. Everyone walks away richer.

V. NIETZSCHE CONTRA MADAME BOVARY

Spiritual nausea conceals the cleverest disguises. Even the mediocre will guess how poor, helpless, arrogant and mistaken these "great poets," men like Byron, are. Wretched minor fiction in a world of paradox, incision, memory. Disguises usually conceal some fracture, a cheerful love affair of the ugly and the horrible. On the whole, a sphere of effects both luxurious, and senseless.

They negate life. Flaubert, for example, tortured himself with ambition, with an excess of procreating, regarding goodness of all kinds as a mouthpiece for his sombre, sick, partly pampered and artificial frenzy. Only the sight of the terrible and the questionable has become creative. At any moment the nooks of collapsed houses will grow in cynical rebellion. The poet, shy amphibian, will dance boldly, exuberantly; with the whole gesture a mere occasion for condescending insights and puerile poses.

The real drama is in the convulsions of history. Whatever is perfect suffers no witnesses.

BIOGRAFFITI

IN MY EXPERIENCE, THE SECOND DATE IS ALWAYS A LETDOWN. I THINK OF MY MOTORCYCLE AS MY BEST FRIEND. GIVEN A CHOICE, I'D RATHER BE WEALTHY THAN HAPPY. TAKE IT FROM ME, LOVE HURTS.

I REALLY SHOULDN'T SAY THIS. IT'S GREAT TO HAVE GOALS, BUT WE'RE NOT SURE YOU HAVE MANAGEMENT POTENTIAL. LET'S JUST TAKE THIS SLOWLY, ONE DAY AT A TIME. FIRST TIME YOU'RE LATE, YOU'RE FIRED.

IT IS BEST NOT TO MAKE YOUR WORK A REFUGE FROM LIFE. TELEVISION SOMETIMES HELPS. AS YOU AGE, EACH YEAR SEEMS HARDER THAN THE LAST. DAY AFTER DAY, EVERYTHING THE SAME.

SOME THINGS ARE DIFFICULT TO DESCRIBE. I'VE OFTEN WONDERED WHAT IT WOULD BE LIKE TO BE JESUS. THE VILLAGES BURNING, THE CHILDREN SCREAMING. BRIGHT WINDOWS, BRIGHT FIRES BURNING.

I'VE ALWAYS HATED SURPRISE
PARTIES. I CAN'T AFFORD TO BE
DEPRESSED RIGHT NOW. I WORRY
ABOUT THE FIRMNESS OF MY
HANDSHAKE. I SECRETLY BELIEVE
I'M SUPERIOR TO EVERYONE.

MY FATHER WARNED ME THIS DAY MIGHT COME. NO BIG SURPRISE THERE. I'VE DONE NOTHING TO BE ASHAMED OF. THERE ARE SOME TIMES WHEN YOU JUST HAVE TO TAKE WHAT'S COMING TO YOU.

WE NEVER GO OUT ANYMORE.
WHEN WE WERE DATING, EVERY
THING WAS MAGIC. I'M AFRAID OF
GROWING OLD, AFRAID OF THE
PHONE. NOTHING SEEMS TO TURN
OUT LIKE YOU HOPED IT WOULD.

I'M JUST NOT SURE HE SEES ME,
YOU KNOW? DO THESE THINGS GO
TOGETHER? SURE, HE TALKS
TOUGH, BUT HE'S A SWEETHEART
UNDER IT ALL REALLY. ARE YOU
SURE I DON'T LOOK FAT IN THIS?

AS A BOY, I STOLE CHANGE FROM MOM'S PURSE. I WAS SO GUILTY I DROPPED IT DOWN A DRAIN. EVERY TIME I FAIL, I FEEL LIKE I DESERVE IT. EVERY TIME I'M PRAISED, I REMEMBER THE MISSING CHANGE.

I ALWAYS CONSIDERED BILLIARDS A SPORT. I'VE SOMETIMES BEEN AROUSED BY FORENSIC PHOTOS. EVEN NOW, MY PARENTS STILL THINK OF ME AS THE BABY. IN MY DREAMS, MY FACE IS AN OCEAN.

a supermodel's
STORY

CHAPTER ONE: TREATISE ON STYLE

Style is a collision of speed and beauty.

Without beauty, style is without purpose, a loud foreign car revving its engine in a locked garage.

Without speed, style is without motivation. Without speed, style is just a beautiful kind of death.

A brick, sitting on the sidewalk, as seen from the window of a hurtling taxi, is a pure object.

A designer watch, caught between the seat cushions of a hurtling taxi, is a waste of swiss craftsmanship.

A designer watch, wrapped around a brick, and hurled through the window of a hurtling taxi, is style.

CHAPTER TWO: SEX

Three women gather near the steps leading up to a clocktower.
"Sex is like fine wine," one of the women offers, "The older it gets,
the drier it is."

The second of of the women steps forward. She wears blue nail
polish and a white rose in her lapel.
"Sex is like fine wine," she says, "the older it gets, the easier it is to
pull the cork."

The third woman is wearing a red hat. She steps backwards into
the shadow cast by the clocktower.
"Sex both is and is not like fine wine," she says, "but I think it most
resembles an injured bird."

Her companions bring their glasses to their lips.

CHAPTER THREE: DISCOURSE ON BEAUTY

Monika remembers being twelve years old. She is taller than the boys in her class, and more awkward than the other girls. Stretch, they call her. Stilts.

"I was an ugly duckling," she confesses to the interviewers. "No one wanted to go out with me."

But this not true. Bobby Thornton wanted to go out with Monika. Bobby Thornton appreciated Monika's inner beauty. He did not care that she was tall and skinny and had no breasts to speak of. Bobby spent many hours imagining what it would be like to touch her cool, white neck, to close his eyes as she bent her slenderness over him and lowered their first kiss to his eager lips.

Bobby Thornton had terrible acne and huge feet. He dressed clumsily, in his older brother's castoffs. Boys tormented him and the girls recoiled when he approached, like he was a snake or a dead thing.

Monika has forgotten about Bobby Thornton and the eloquent testimonials he left in her locker, written with love in his cramped, respectful hand. She tells the interviewers she was an ugly duckling.

CHAPTER FOUR: TRACTUS PHILOSOPHICUS

Monika and Brittany look at life in two very different ways. Monika sees the universe as a vast and unfathomable place, ruled equally by awkward logic and random, indiscriminate violence. Monika sees each solar system and galaxy as representing only a tiny grain on a vast, endless celestial beach. In such a cosmos, she reasons, what does it matter what crimes and catastrophes are visited on individual planets or on the puny souls which inhabit them? Our lives are like dust motes, barely visible and unnoticed, falling endlessly through infinity's indifferent gaze.

Brittany thinks it works better from the inside out. If you believe the universe is cold and lonely, that our lives are like ice cubes, thrown from the deck of a luxury cruise ship, only to melt into the vastness of the cosmic sea, then that is the reality you have made, and the reality that you deserve. Like Sartre, Brittany believes in individual responsibility. So what if the universe is cold and lonely and indifferent, that there is no force which is inherently good or inherently hostile. We must accept responsibility for the footprints we leave, however modest the footfall, however soft the sole. Small stones leave vast ripples, she tells her friend.

Monika says we must face our irrelevance. Brittany says irrelevance is an illusion. Each feels the other's view to be misguided, though not entirely without merit.

CHAPTER FIVE: MONIKA'S DREAM

Monika dreams she is on a vast, purple slope. At the top of the slope, partially obscured by the morning mist, is a sign advertising a fast food joint which must lie beyond the crest of the hill. To her right, a multitude of cowed men and women from all walks of life snake their way towards the summit. Each carries a polystyrene package containing a partially eaten food item. Monika moves closer to see what it is, joining for the moment the sullen line which trudges, three abreast, upwards. She can see now that the contents of the package is the same in every case: a soggy hamburger, with one bite missing. A long, noticeably curly black hair protrudes from the middle of each burger, at the point where the bite has been taken.

Monika looks down at her own hands, which hold a similar polystrene package. Steam rises as she opens the lid, and takes a bite of the perfect burger which lies inside. As she lowers the burger from her lips she feels a momentary tug of resistance. When she looks down at what remains, she sees a dark curly hair protruding from the bun. She turns to the man next to her, a weary looking businessman in an ill-fitted suit.

"Imagine the odds against THAT happening!" she says.

CHAPTER SIX: DISCOURSE ON MECHANICS

Speed creates pure objects. There are moments when the banana daiquiri mix is a Platonic yellow as it slushes over the inner surface of Monika's blender. An ideal yellow, like the ones you see in children's books. On the highway, we pass the same farmhouse a thousand times, and, like Fred Flintstone locked in the logic of an infinitely large stone age livingroom, we will be unable to distinguish one from another. And yet Monika knows they must all be different, that there are whispers unique to each room in each farmhouse, that no two men and women work the instruments of their toil in exactly the same way. Monika suspects that each soul in each flesh house carries something original and painful and unexposed, trickling like an inner wound. She reasons that while speed creates pure objects, they are objects speed does not understand.

Monika knows that at some undeniable level, speed cannot be trusted.

CHAPTER SEVEN: DEATH

Monika is only slightly afraid that death might overtake her before she has accomplished everything she has set out to do in life. She sees contradiction in the ways people work toward long-term goals, work to an abstract creed of perfectability, and in the ways death works against such notions. Sometimes Monika sees life as a rehearsal for death, an expensive, well-mounted production of a half-finished opera, for which death will serve as an unannounced finale. Monika is not as afraid of death as she is of this life-play, afraid that it will go on forever, the players improvising valiantly beyond the script, death hanging over the proceedings, the ever-promised, ever-postponed relief from an interminable one-act tragedy.

Think of death, Monika says, as a heavy backdrop, collapsing on the diva.

Think of death as an intermission that never ends, with free drinks for everyone.

Think of death as a hard, driving wind, howling over the copper roof of the opera-house in a voice both wild and plaintive, a voice so compelling that the performers pause, and the musicians lift their lips from their instruments so that they too can listen.

Think of death as the audience rising silently, and the extras slipping in from the wings, and everyone in the theatre looking up into the eaves, listening for their names in the midst of all that terrible shouting.

arbitrary
CULTURES

I WAS A TEENAGED HATBAND

We could see the brou-ha-ha in the square
from where we sat, percolating in the café
in the gold sun, eager lizards licking the atmosphere
of rage.

The bullets popped and snapped like brass bands
on a 3-nite luxury hotel excursion (breakfast
included), as the blood expelled its warm
whippet into the agitated current of full-scale
revolution.

"What swift disappearance, what newspaper anonymity,"
the lemon twists remark, raising
identically pristine, gasping pinkies,
ribbing the dreams of our grandparents with
third generation shoo-be-doo fifth avenue
hair-dos, swept garishly across the bursting rose
of the face, a break with etiquette
ill-appreciated in Tucson.

CHARIOTS OF THE GODS

They do not speak and they have no desire.
They have their own newspapers,
an obscure laboratory in Mexico City,
an élite handful of the major players
to influence observers of the media.

Life, and her darling oddball, the air,
are becoming increasingly beautiful.

A BRIEF HISTORY OF LIGHT

The real wild card here
is Thomas Edison,
a complex, attractive hero
and the patent office that inspired him.

His young wife
married the football hero,
a fan's approach to science.
No one would disagree
that his life has been
forceful, flowing,
a new role model for being.

Edison says that
sound, during its birth,
was a finite place
filled with the names of cities,
spaces in which his recollections
could use accents for comic emphasis.

The light bulb was not
a TV and an automobile,
an upper middle class neighbourhood,
the good life.

The future, a usually quiet,
overpriced restaurant,
becomes a remarkably tiny cadre
of terms with memories,
confidential documents and correspondence;

a brilliant fable
offering the steps needed to make
the next necessary breakthrough.

The bulb winks,
a mixed blessing
conducting seminars in major cities
for the next twenty years.

He tries to penetrate its
gruesome secret, to arouse
his consuming desire for Isabel,
a married woman.
His guilt feelings,
concubinage and gambling,
the odor of cyanide and despair.

While Edison lived
lightbulbs were immortal.
Now, in the smooth halls
they die hourly in his honor.

ARBITRARY CULTURES

What do you think is
meant by "a healthy dose?"
Sour clouds are spilling
against the metal hills
like stained bees
spinning to a stop
against a window screen.

I'm sure you'll be impressed
when I tell you the vines
have split, gnawed themselves
off at the root and blown away.

The lights go on at Wrigley Field;
a world resigns itself to shallow desperation.
Phonographs are shouting dance
dance dance dance dance-to-the-radio,
and I guess there's sense in that.
The lilies tremble under the aquaducts,
night sharpens its knuckles on the hot asphalt.

We will make the best of these mistakes:
settle on the secret ingredients,
rearrange the rubbled cities
into quaint cliffside towns.

We will put our shoulders
to the grim bluff of science,
repopulate ourselves
one street at a time.

TOO GOOD FOR THE ROOM

When I use the word
"sleepless," I imagine
a troubled person
staying up for many nights.

"Chess" is a set of carved
men, and the box they go in.

"Syncopation" conjures
images of a coconut
and a stone—and something
suitable for striking both.

For a change of pace
I settle on "funeral",
the starched invitation,
requests for replies about
the optional buffet.

I have grapes for eyes—in place
of fingers: rolled slices of ham.
My stomach is a punchbowl, rippling
under a gaggle of strangers
praising my colouring.

I make a note
to take all the strangers
off my mailing list.

THE SWIMMER, THE DRUGSTORE, THE PAINTED WORDS

Dawn cordons the walkways
with shadows, helps the litter
up out of the gutter so it
can throw itself on the feet
of passing girls, riding
on the cuffs and begging
for a kiss, a handout,
a bit of free advice.

Her hair is wet and she trudges
up the alley and past
the closed drugstore.
The day is blinding,
the kind of bright
that makes everything flat
and shocking and ready for breakfast.

It's as if someone has had
the words scrubbed overnight,
stood them in line with the hydrants
and the row houses like empty cells,
spaces we're required to fill, individually.
For some they will be uniform,
the edges traced carefully
with the tongue;

others, like the swimmer's,
rushed and sloppy,
because she is strong,
and busy with her own grace.

ALARMS

You expected all this
would stay the same,
at least in your head,
at least in the things
you clutched and guarded.
But even there it's messed up,
unoccupied, bricked over
and settling into death
like frozen runners,
or the set alarms on
all the stopped clocks
in the jewellery shop.

You could recite something,
a mnemonic, maybe find
a word in your pocket
that might help.
But memory stumbles,
religiously, over itself,
chasing its demise
like a younger brother,
overbundled and scrabbling,
abandoned on the ice.

The darkness you spilled
on the evening is running
out toward the edges in a wave.
You paw at it, try to turn
the motion back, the tiny
differences ringing free

of one another already,
underneath the dark
stutter of a
clotted heart.

PROOF

Object lesson: Take a piece of clay
and roll it between your fingers.
Try not to create a responsibility.

You know these feelings brought about
by twilight and venetian blinds
but, please, let's not go into them.
The end is tiresome, and the motives suspect.

"You have nothing to prove in this lifetime,"
she said, undermining everything with her pressed skirt.

My life is dissolving like this fine line,
in time, I hope, without thought
or purposed smiling.
My eyes tear, but refuse to drop.
I have tried, but have no style for weeping,
for releasing the incumbent image.

I have found ways to take time
from my neighbour's tennis game;
I have taken liberties with silence,
kept company with sailors.
In short, I have played the good fellow,
juggled the odd moment
and dropped the even ones.

I have seen faces
across the long green park;
imagined the gazebo,

edited the orchestra
to a single, rude instrument:
a tuba, an elbow perhaps.

Listen to the voices out beyond the river.
"Bravo!" they shout, "Good show,
Continue by all means."
I've lingered by this river
waiting for the sun
to sing the wet tree's diamond,
then buckled, found some quaint escape.

I empty my drawers, calculate the response.
Soft ... wait for it ....

PROGRESS REPORT

The way the rain runs up the street
afraid of drowning,
the spitting roof tipped below the
window as I take my seat.
Today, my legs are broccoli-coloured.
I have webbed feet.
Pinned open on the kidney tray
I wait for a nervous student
to misidentify my pancreas.

The rain gusts and turns the windows
into Woolworth's soda fountains.
Trees jump back from a moving street
like startled chickens;
the leaves quiver,
silver arrows pointing
at a stunned sky.

I have a memory like this:
out the back of the house
as a child, watching the storm
roll over the field, hanging
on the silo of the vacant farm,

the odd bird shouting at the grass,
and gusts of wind actually
blowing through my head,
leaving it sharp
and crisp as an apple.

My life, at worst, has been conducted in
a light drizzle. Though I have seen two
plane crashes ... one only tall flames
at the village airport, the other
a Blue Angel at the Ex—
his wing dipped a teaspoon from the lake
and he was gone in a cough of flame.

When he was in the airforce
Dad bailed out over Quebec,
but he was back in three days
with only a frightened wife
and insect bites to contend with.

Nothing very dramatic has happened since—
a couple of car accidents, couple
of people I didn't know much dying.
School. Two pennant races,
a few shit jobs.

Even the rain's not very dramatic.
It couldn't put out the
fire on that pilot's airsuit.
It can't even get through
a thin wall of glass.

Still, it pushes you inside
and breathes on you,
messing up the order of a few years,
forcing a little long grass
up through the bald lawns of
what is now suburbia.

It hangs over the drawer
of my short life putting
wrong things together:
a hammer and two screws,
a ball of string and an
unmailed letter,
an eraser and a matchbook—

small, useful things I keep,
but have no home for.

NOTES ON THE TEXT

"They Remain Hatless," "Raw Dough," and "Bernie's Tears" were
developed from titles supplied by Stuart Ross. The brief quota-
tions in "Twelve Arrests, No Convictions" are taken, respectively,
from David Byrne's "Born Under Punches," and John
Berryman's poem "He Resigns" (1972).

"Chariots of The Gods," and "A Brief History of Light" were com-
posed using the surrealist cut-up technique.

The poems in "Notes Towards a Revised Biography of Friedrich
Nietzsche" collage words and phrases from Nietzsche, recombin-
ing them to form texts whose meanings veer sharply from those
of the source texts.

Born in Biloxi, Mississippi, Kevin Connolly has spent most of his life in Toronto, where he works as a poet, editor, critic and fiction writer.

As a critic, his work has appeared in *Brick, The Toronto Star, Books in Canada, This Magazine* and *The MacMillan Anthology.*

He was co-founder and co-editor from 1985-1993 (with Jason Sherman) of the influential literary magazine *WHAT!,* and now serves as arts editor of *This Magazine.* A veteran of the Toronto small press scene, Connolly edits the Pink Dog chapbook series, which has featured a number of the city's best young writers.

Editor for the Press: Lynn Crosbie
Author photograph: Gil Adamson

Coach House Press
50 Prince Arthur Ave. #107
Toronto, Canada M5R 1B5